Taming the Anger Monster

Om KIDZ
An imprint of Om Books International

Bang! Crack! Smash!

All the children watched in dismay, as the muddy football sailed through the air. It smashed Mrs. Penny's kitchen window and landed right on top of her beautiful apple pie. The pie was destroyed, so was the kitchen table and the floor. The room was covered in glass shards.

Oh boy! Emma was in big trouble now.

This was the second time this week she'd broken something in anger!

None of the children in the playground waited to find out what happened next. Everyone ran for cover! Emma ran, too.

'Why? Oh why can't I stop myself from getting mad?' She mumbled to herself.

She knew there would be trouble at home. Mrs Penny's neighbour had seen her kick the football. He had been watching their game.

'If only I hadn't lost my head at Ben's teasing,' she thought.

Emma came home to find Mommy and Daddy waiting for her. Their grim faces told her that they knew everything.

'I'm very disappointed, Emma,' said Daddy in a firm voice. 'You are grounded for a week.'

`But Daddy, I can explain,' Emma began. They had a football match next Wednesday. She could not possibly miss it!

`Young lady, you promised not to cause any trouble on Monday,' said Mother. `That's twice in three days. How do you explain that?'

Emma went up to her room to find Grandpa waiting for her. `It's all Ben's fault!' She cried, flinging her cap violently to the floor.

`What did Ben do?´ Grandpa asked.

`Oh Grandpa!´ Said Emma in relief. She could tell him everything.

`Why, he kept teasing me. He said I couldn´t kick the ball far enough, because I´m only a girl!´ Emma was getting angry again.

`Calm down, sweetheart, take a deep breath, and look at me.´

'I know how you're feeling, Emma. When I was your age, I used to get very angry, too. I would break things and hurt people.'

'Really?' Emma asked in surprise. She could not imagine Grandpa as an angry little boy.

'But you never get mad. You're always so calm!'

'That's because I know a little trick. Would you like to learn it?'

Emma nodded eagerly.

'Well, whenever you get angry, you have to remember three things.'

`First, stop and breathe deeply. As many times as your age.´

`I'm seven! I'll breathe deeply seven times,´ said Emma excitedly.

`That's right, dear. Second, open up your palms and place them in front of you. When you're angry, your fingers curl into fists.´

`And I feel like breaking something or hurting someone!'

`Stop that feeling and look at your hands,' said Grandpa kindly.

`And third?' Emma asked.

`Say "I'm not angry" loudly and slowly. As many times as your age.'

Emma got a chance to practice Grandpa's advice the very next day.

In school, Ben began to tease her again, as usual.

'I bet you got into trouble yesterday. I told you, girls are no good at football!' He laughed.

Emma felt the familiar feeling of anger. But she remembered the three little tricks.

She breathed in and out, slowly. Seven times.
Then she uncurled her fists and looked at her hands.

'I'm not angry,' she said aloud. Slowly repeating the words twice, thrice, four times...

Emma had closed her eyes, trying hard to calm down. When she opened her eyes, her anger had disappeared. It was magic!

All her friends stood around, looking at her in surprise. Emma did not push Ben or throw anything at him. She stood there smiling, instead.

Emma had learnt a new trick!

The whole class clapped. They were proud of Emma.

As a special treat, Mrs. Jones, her class teacher, spoke to Emma's parents about the football match.

Emma would be playing after all!